How to Create a VIBRANT CULTURE in Uncertain Times

JACK PACHUTA

Paperback
ISBN 978-1-888475-12-8

Hard Cover
ISBN 978-1-888475-35-7

FOURTH EDITION

About the Cover

Why are storm clouds on the cover? After all, this book is about people and about how they function within organizations.

The cover artwork went through several generations, from nondescript graphic to a shadowy photo of people walking near each other without recognition or emotion. None of them relayed the message I was looking for.

Finally, as I walked home beneath a dreary, stormy sky, it became apparent that the sky said it all. COVID-19, political polarization, a global economic downturn and a military crisis in Eastern Europe have created gloom that encircled the world.

It's difficult to navigate paths in stormy economic, political and social environments – both for businesses and for individuals. And the strategies for making it through these storms require clear options and the judgment to select and implement the correct ones.

Yet, with the proper skill and the ability to make adjustments, the storm might not entirely blow away, but can be readily placed in the proper context. Through the figurative chaos of lightning and confusion of thunder, people and organizations can emerge, if not unscathed, at least stronger and more resilient for undergoing the hectic experience.

With the right plan - and the knowledge and ability to carry it out - the storm can be a valuable learning life-changing experience with a long-term positive impact.

In this book, I'll give you my perspectives about the course your organization might be taking and ideas about how to make it through the storm when the times are tough. After all, it's easy to make decisions on a clear day. When the storms hit, your job gets a lot more difficult!

JP

Dedication

This book is dedicated to my friend and deceased colleague T Frank Hardesty. I met Frank in 1979 when I was hired to be the first-ever training manager at a financial service company in Milwaukee. At that time, Frank was a seasoned veteran in many ways. In his pedigree (he didn't have a resume), he referred to the fact that he'd fought at Iwo Jima, ("We won") but not to the fact that he'd never finished high school.

He'd advanced up the corporate ladder through street smarts and determination, and was then a "director" of the company – more out of convenience than out of necessity.

Frank was a self-educated person whose insightful observations led him to a successful career as a speaker and consultant before anyone really knew what that was. I learned much about how to handle an audience and communicate a message by being around Frank. Even today, I still use some of his material. (I have his permission to do so), and yes, I am still asked about him.

His influence runs rampant in this book – and he could have written a similar one if he'd had the mind to do it. Frank was my first true mentor in the art of working with people. I shall forever be grateful for the time I spent with him.

Contents

Introduction
Unique in their similarities

Y ou've felt it. We all have. A brief walk-through gives you a sense, a feel for how a company functions. You don't have distinct, defined reasons for those feelings. You only know that you already understand something about how that organization operates. In recent decades, this functioning has been labeled **organizational culture.** Each one is as distinct and personal as an ethnic or a family culture.

They vary among companies and organizations, and are determined by the ways in which their members interact, decisions are made, and rewards are given. Individual success within these cultures depends upon the ability to identify the clues that categorize the people, moods, and emotions that are part of the entire structure.

Then, an individual can resolve personal uncertainties by either developing a strategy for coping or, sad as it may seem, by fleeing to another organization where the culture is more in-line with personal values, beliefs and methods of operations.

What This Book IS NOT

This book is *not* an academic exercise or scientific study filled with charts, diagrams and calculated proofs that what I'm writing shouldn't be challenged. It was never my intent to compile numbers and calculations into a system that would be more at home on a spread sheet than on a bookshelf. Certainly, I've used those types of studies when I needed specific insights into a particular area. They can be valuable tools to pinpoint paths that potentially can be explored.

Yet, documents that are too focused on the numbers often neglect the fundamental issue that I address in this book. It is people that make any organization vibrant and successful. By understanding what is *really* happening in the hearts and minds of its people, an organization is better equipped to handle today's global marketplace, especially when supply chains are interrupted and public health issues can quickly create unexpected roadblocks.

What This Book IS

This book is a collection of true-life anecdotes that I observed and lived as a corporate player, trainer, and consultant. They are not quantifiable as formulas or unalterable projections. Instead, they are my ramblings about the more than three decades that I've spent working with people in many organizations in various capacities.

It is no different than inviting you to sit down at my kitchen table, have a cup of coffee and just talk about what I've been doing. Over the years, many of my clients have told me that this is what's been most valuable to them – the opportunity to pick my brain and discuss what I've observed while getting involved in their operations.

So, this book gives you that personal, intimate perspective that isn't always shared unless it is requested. While I can't always tell you why I think and feel the way that I do, I would argue those thoughts and feelings are as valid (sometimes even more valid) as many of the academic studies that attempt to quantify with precision what goes on in the corporate world.

As much as managers and executives like to depend upon hard facts to make decisions, a simple truth is that people don't always fit into the same flowcharts and graphs that are analyzed during board meetings and investor briefings. The people in any organization need to be looked at in a different way.

The World Is Changing

During the '90s, the world economy was in its period of historic prosperity and organizations felt they had all the answers for success in a growing global marketplace.

On the morning of September 11, 2001, I was sharing some of the concepts that are the foundation for this book with an annual meeting of business professionals in Pewaukee, Wisconsin. After my presentation, the group's president announced that the nation was under terrorist attack.

That's when the words "uncertain times" were added to the title of this book. In retrospect, though, the uncertain times didn't start or stop then. The events of that day certainly added a new dimension to the uncertainty, but the ebb of the business cycle had started 18 months earlier.

Seven years later, in September of 2008, the nation and the world found out that letting the fox guard the henhouse wasn't a way to ensure long-term, global prosperity. The world economy stalled and drastic measures were required to put it back on course.

A struggle in Afghanistan and a massive oil spill in the Gulf of Mexico, coupled with a refusal in some quarters to admit that corporations should be fully responsible for their actions, all played into how an organizational culture affects the entire global community.

Economic conditions then improved and world financial markets rebounded. Yet, the scars from those events remained a constant reminder of what can happen when the collective attention lapses into complacency.

With the war in Ukraine and the return of worldwide inflation, coupled with a crisis in the fossil fuel industry and a continuing pandemic, the goblins of uncertainty returned, and once again, a plan with realistic options is required to weather the storm.

Throughout the years, a consistent theme in working with my clients has been that "good people" are hard to find. Even when unemployment figures are high, it's still difficult to match the person with the job. So, though this book takes special note of the dynamics of the new world economy, the observations and principles that you'll find in its pages apply to all times.

Frank Hardesty used to point out that nothing is new in management theory except the name we give to the latest "hot" concept. While I used to smile when he said it, in retrospect he knew exactly what he was saying.

New theories ebb and recede like an endless tide lapping at the organizational shore. The constant, though, is the people who populate the structure. Their feelings and attitudes are at the core of everything that is done and achieved.

What you'll find here is a system for looking at an organization based upon the attitudes of top management, the roles played by its members, and the operating philosophy that permeates all levels. The stories shared in this book really happened. The actual companies in which they took place will go unnamed. You'll see the American corporate world through my eyes, and be privy to the thought processes that led to my conclusions.

They provide a starting point for understanding and initiating potential reform. They could also predict an impending organizational death as viability can be questioned and scrutinized in light of an organization's workings. As with the human condition, most causes of death are internal and endemic. They are long, slow illnesses which manifest themselves over a period of time. Without treatment, they can be terminal.

Although this book focuses on corporate America, the concepts and conclusions apply to all institutions in which people attempt to work together to achieve common goals.

My colleagues in the field of consulting will confirm that all organizations have a great deal of similarity in the ways in which they function, but within those similarities are the variations which make cultures unique. In that regard, the terms "company" and "organization" are, for the most part, interchangeable in this book.

By quantifying the similarities and the differences, I attempt to put culture into perspective and enable a quick diagnosis, leading to prescriptions that remedy potential problems. The choice either to take the medicine or to continue along the same path remains with the organization itself.

Today, the world operates in an environment in which opportunities are tempered by world events and uncertain futures. Email, texting and worldwide video conferencing puts added pressure on decision-makers to get it right the first time. Organizations now deal with a new set of challenges and a need for accelerated change. Progressive organizations with vibrant cultures will survive. The others will not.

Chapter 1
The Basics
What culture is all about

The first step in understanding what's happening is to observe what's going on in the world around us. When patterns and results repeat over time with high degrees of predictability, we have a basis for making statements that can be accepted as true. Trained researchers are good observers who translate what they've seen into theories and laws before taking action.

In the same way, my consulting and training engagements have given me the rare chance to observe the inner workings of many organizations. And, as with scientific researchers, I've tracked the repetition of patterns in how organizations function. Consultants like to think that they are intuitive, and that their suggestions are based upon an almost-mystical process.

Consultants, though, merely translate prior experiences into logical projections of what is likely to happen in the future. The many observations I've stored in my gray matter data base are condensed here into what I call *The Basics*. That term is a tongue-in-cheek reference to the way in which many organizations approach their problem-solving sessions.

How often have you said or have you heard other people say, "We've got to get back to basics"? Most often, they mean they've got to return to the operational philosophies that worked in the past. The fallacy is, of course, that in today's marketplace the basics have changed and continue to change. And, since the Septembers of 2001 and 2008, and the pandemic of 2019, new items have been added to the list of "must-have" considerations for success.

As a controversial presidency ended and the New York Stock Exchange reached its highest levels in history, companies around the world took a renewed look at their leaders and at the people who populate all levels of the organizational structure. Some dramatic management changes were the result, as well as major course corrections.

In this book, *The Basics* establish the ground rules for a perspective on organizational culture. They are not complicated. Most people will nod their heads in agreement as they are given, reinforcing the simple truth that organizational culture is easy to observe.

It's not the observations, but how they are used that determines success. Utilization reaches to the very core of the attitudes and beliefs that support any group. These attitudes and beliefs help determine when changes must be made and the strategies that must be implemented for meaningful change to occur.

Belief systems hold revered positions in most organizations. They are the sacred cows that roam the streets and are left unchallenged no matter what happens. Often, they are locked into the structure to such a degree that any attempt to revisit or change them is viewed as naivety or disloyalty. Yet, many core beliefs no longer reflect the world or the marketplace. Still, they intertwine with everything the organization does and can lead decision-makers down the wrong paths.

It is not always easy to make course modifications to an organizational ship that may be steaming in the wrong direction. I am told that it takes five to eight nautical miles to turn an ocean liner totally around. This turning radius is small when compared to what it takes to turn some companies around and to realize the effects of their current belief system and their stated long-range objectives.

The next chapters examine The Basics one at a time. Their impact is pervasive and at the heart of all successes or failures.

Chapter 2
The Executive Thumbprint
It all starts at the top

L eaders imprint their organizations with values, beliefs and operational philosophies. A brief conversation with the person (or people) at the top will tell you much about how people at all levels of the organization are expected to think and feel. So, then, here's Basic #1:

Basic #1: *The person at the top of the organization sets the tone for the way in which the entire organization functions.*

Whether for good or for ill, top management marks the organization with a thumbprint that affects everyone on the staff. Individuals who join the workforce with divergent opinions soon feel the pressure to adapt to the chief executive's perspective. No one is overtly told to alter their opinions, but it soon becomes apparent that "that's what we believe."

Those who do buy in are promoted. Those who do not, are left to stagnate with no advancement potential. It goes to the very core of the operational methods and attitudes that support any organization.

When the philosophy from above is one of openness, employees feel a sense of community and importance. If however, top management is closed and clandestine in its dealings, employees adopt similar patterns of intrigue and game-playing.

While some chief executives revel in the ability to form the organization in their own images, others are oblivious to the behind-the-scenes power that they have. Either they have been in their positions so long that they take these dynamics for granted, or they do not understand that "do as I say, not as I do" has never worked as a management method because employees invariably, in subtle ways, "do as you do."

It is a continuing frustration to me to deal with chief executives who want something done, but who don't want to get involved in doing it. The most critical example of this is the formulation and implementation of an organization's mission and vision.

Many organizations have missions and visions, but only a fraction of them truly live them.

This is one of my hot topics and is discussed in a later chapter, so I'll wait until then to tell you what I *really* think about them.

Commitments to current management theory often seem like frozen custard stands advertising "the flavor of the day." Who can ever forget TQM, or quality circles, or

MBO? In their days, they were held up as solutions to everything that ails an organization.

Many executives embrace the latest buzzwords because they want their organizations to be viewed as being on the cutting edge of management philosophy. Today, with the internet, global networks, and instantaneous news coverage, information moves quickly and tenaciously. (Who can ever forget watching the first bombs strike Baghdad or observing the "Arab Spring" as crowds demonstrated in the Middle East live on television and the Internet? And of course, the events of January 6, 2021 are indelibly imprinted on our brains.)

The marketplace knows who really believes what they say and who are merely mouthing the words.

Often, top management decides to "buy" the latest trend. "Experts" are retained to come in, work with staff, and to leave only when an organization has the external trappings of the new belief system. Consultants can only point out the path to take. They can't implement needed long-term changes without executive support.

When the executives' total involvement in the process is periodic updates or 15-minute briefings of how things are shaping up, staffs are often irritated when the experts leave and nothing has changed. Their bottom lines have not improved and their people have returned to old patterns.

Yet, they still speak the language of the new marketplace because the world requires that they adopt the "in" vocabulary. They are responding to a market demand while not buying into the program.

Take the case of a small service company with which I once worked. The owner used all of the right words when it came to empowerment and employee involvement, but little things tell a lot about a person's real feelings.

Signs in the Lunchroom

One day, I walked into the lunchroom and noticed that the owner had put up a sign. It was a photocopy of a photocopy of a photocopy, so the quality wasn't very good, but the words on the sign spoke volumes about his management style.

The sign read: THE FLOGGINGS WILL CONTINUE UNTIL MORALE IMPROVES. It was the only sign in the entire office that had been personally posted by him.

Not wanting to overreact, I questioned the owner about the sign. He assured me that his people knew him well enough to accept it as the joke it was intended to be. He proclaimed not to subscribe to this philosophy, but found a great deal of humor in the message.

Surreptitiously, I asked the employees about the sign. In general, the response I received was a rolling of the eyes with no spoken comment. That is except for one person who said that she understood how the staff could be offended by the wording, especially since the owner made a point of emphasizing that the company's goal was to treat everyone fairly and equitably.

I approached the owner again and made my case for changing the message. He didn't totally agree with me, but said that he would do something about it.

The next day, I walked into the lunchroom and the sign had been removed. In its place was a handwritten sign asking: ARE WE HAVING FUN YET? This was an improvement, but not what I ultimately had in mind. However, at least the owner was now thinking about the subtle nuances of what he was saying to his staff.

Talk is not only cheap, but also meaningless when other indicators suggest that spoken words aren't supported by internal commitments.

Data Plates Can Communicate A Lot

Contrast that to the case of an international heavy equipment manufacturer whose president became fully immersed in communicating with his staff. After several small group discussions, he realized that plant workers felt divorced from customers.

When a piece of equipment was manufactured and delivered, the people who fabricated the equipment had no contact with the end-users. Any comments or complaints were filtered through sales and customer service personnel who didn't provide effective feedback.

To remedy this, the president encouraged more employee involvement with customers by changing the company's way of doing business. Data plates on the equipment were enlarged. The names of every employee on the work team whose efforts went into producing the final piece of equipment were engraved on the plate. The record stayed with that unit for its lifetime.

Plus, several weeks after delivery, one of the employees named on the plate called the customer and asked a series of questions related to design, satisfaction, and service. Prior to this process, the people who produced the equipment had no contact with the people who used the equipment.

Needless to say, the personal contact had a series of very desirable results. First, the customer was able to ask questions of the work team that could not be answered by either customer service or sales personnel.

Second, the work team received real opinions and feedback about its efforts that translated into pride of ownership and better quality work.

Third, the president of the company proved that his commitment to open the channels of communications was more than just words. It was supported by actions that had a positive impact upon the entire company.

Change can require a cultural shift and a new belief system. Involvement from all levels of the organization is essential.

Lip service does not substitute for conviction. Yet, some top managers believe that they can forego empowering their subordinates and still be successful. Top managers may not always say this overtly, but by their actions and through their failure to "walk the talk," they reveal their true inner opinions.

Chapter 3
Talk to the Right Person
Finding the solution is simple

Ask any consultant how to come up with a solution in a relatively short period of time. If honest, the consultant will share a simple, yet effective, strategy. The secret is to find the person who is closest to the problem and who already knows the answer. Then, ask that person to solve the problem.

Frequently, that person has been waiting to share this solution with a decision-maker, but hasn't been asked for input. Basic #2, then, is:

> **Basic #2:** *Someone within the organization has the solution to every perceived problem of the organization.*

Why don't employees share ideas and solutions with the decision-makers in a company? The answer is different depending on the organization, but many of the answers relate to established patterns of reward and reaction.

What happened in the past when an employee did offer an insight or an opinion? If positive feedback was given and the employee was made to feel good about the process, then openness and communication become patterns, and eventually habits within the organization. If the employee received negative vibes for even offering a suggestion, potential solutions went undercover and everyone lost.

The Real Experts

While working on a project with a major organization on the East Coast, I was analyzing the flow of information within the company. My trail of data led me to a department that was involved in the process. The department's staff mentioned several reports that seemed to compile duplicate or insignificant information. They seemed frustrated.

"We've been telling our manager about it for months," was the response, "but he won't listen to us. Since they're paying you a lot of money to do this, maybe someone will listen to you."

Later that day, I pointed out the same duplication to a senior vice president. She was unaware that the reports were wasting staff time and organizational money. The comments of the people closest to the situation hadn't gotten farther than the department manager who chose to operate in a way that wouldn't rock the boat.

The problem would have been solved months before if only someone had paid attention to the real experts in the organization, the people who must deal with the work flow daily.

The Suggestion Box

Another client once decided to solicit the untapped knowledge within the organization by placing a suggestion box in a prominent position in the headquarters building. Anyone could submit suggestions that, in theory, would change the way in which the company operated.

The first week that the box appeared, it was filled with ideas. Management was pleased that its concept of employee involvement was working, but in its view, found very little in the suggestions that was useful. However, the box was maintained because it provided an outlet for employees and (thought management) a good idea might eventually be submitted.

The second week brought fewer suggestions, and subsequent weeks saw the numbers decrease even further. "Why," asked management, "aren't the employees continuing to take this chance to give us their ideas? We're doing our part, but they're not doing theirs."

After about a month, submissions to the box had almost dried up and, in their place, management began to find rude notes that complained about conditions without making any constructive recommendations for improvement. Within two months, the box was gone.

"See," said management, "this just shows you what can happen when you overestimate the workforce. We knew it wouldn't work."

The problem, of course, rested in the dichotomy between theory and practice. Management told employees that the suggestions would improve the workplace. Yet, none of the suggestions were either acknowledged or implemented.

Over time, employees felt that they had been duped, that nothing would change as a result of their ideas. In an attempt to give only superficial lip service to employee involvement, management had created a monster that confirmed to employees that the top really didn't care what other levels of the company had to say.

To encourage the people with the solutions to speak up, an organization must create a culture that fosters and rewards new ideas, even if the ideas can't realistically be implemented, or if they are different than management's solutions.

Actions must be taken which indicate that an individual's input was considered and valued. In uncertain times, the credibility of the messenger is critical. If the person who formulates the words isn't regarded as someone who should be believed, not only does the message fall on deaf ears, but it could also be considered laughable by those to whom the message is directed. I had a personal experience in which I attempted to circumvent this reaction before it ever occurred.

Why should I believe you?

One of my first assignments when entering the corporate world was to design a training program for line employees. Although I had the writing and research skills to do the job, I had never actually performed the duties that I was expected to formalize. I needed to quickly make myself knowledgeable in the content area.

How, I thought, could I get the "doers" to believe that someone who had never done the job could train other people to do it? My strategy was this. I found five corporate staff members who were regarded as experts by their peers and subordinates. They became my advisors.

Through a series of reviews and revisions, I used their ideas to develop the program. In reality, my initial research had pinpointed 90% of the necessary content. But, their 10% supplied the credibility that I required. By making a conscious effort to include comments and techniques from all five advisors in the final version of the training, I created a buy-in.

Because they all felt ownership, they helped me sell the program to the rest of the corporation. I had, in a very real way, created an internal sales staff that would use its power and influence to ensure that the training material would be utilized and supported.

When a buy-in exists and people feel that they are being heard, solutions multiply in both quantity and frequency.

In addition, the individuals whose ideas have been implemented become advocates of the changes and, by osmosis, of the company's method of operation.

Chapter 4
What Do You Expect from Me?
Job descriptions aren't the answer

Realizing the emphasis placed by many organizations in formalized job descriptions, I can't help but smile when I see one that was written in the not-too-distant past, but which no longer applies because of changes in the staff and in the operating philosophy. Note Basic #3:

> **Basic #3:** *An organization's work distribution and communication channels adapt to the individuals who join and leave an organization.*

Organizations are living, growing entities. As the people within an organization develop and mature, come and go, the internal channels and job responsibilities are revised.

Job Descriptions

A job description is a snapshot of a position at a particular point in time. Just as people change over time, jobs change over time. We do not expect our family portraits to look the same from year to year, yet many corporate managers and executives demand that their people be placed into boxes that are either unalterable or which no longer apply.

Unfortunately, once job descriptions are written, they seem to hang around organizations for a long time. And, they serve mainly to define what employees do *not* do. How often have you heard someone in your organization say, "That's not in my job description?" Infrequently you may hear someone say, "Okay, that *is* in my job description."

I'll wager, though, that you have never heard an employee or coworker say, "That's not in my job description, but it *should* be." The nature of these descriptions is to be exclusionary. By their very existence, they limit individual duties and responsibilities and help to stifle some of the creativity that is vital to organizational growth.

Let me again take this situation to a personal level. During my time as a corporate manager, I participated in a company-wide process that instituted job descriptions for all employees. The "all," of course, excluded the people at the top who knew what their jobs were. It was only the rest of us who had to define our roles within the corporate structure.

My departmental staff and I filled out the worksheets and the numerical evaluations that were fed into a system of classifications and pay grades. From that point on, a portion of my time as a manager was spent trying to change the descriptions. The reason: the responsibilities of my department evolved as the company changed. The job descriptions never seemed to catch up with the current situation.

Some of my employees left the department and were replaced with individuals whose talents and strengths were different than those of the people for whom the job descriptions had been written.

As a result, I reassigned duties among my staff members to fit the current composition of the department. And, I created new responsibilities based upon new departmental requirements.

Within a year, the job descriptions were meaningless because they were no longer a true reflection of the people who were filling those jobs. Yet, I was still forced to hire and promote people based upon a list of duties and "expected outcomes" which had, through a natural growth process, changed.

The Thoroughbred Theory

My analogy to the process of developing job descriptions is to take a picture of a thoroughbred racehorse as it speeds around the track. If the photograph is snapped at just the right time, all four of the horse's hooves will be off the ground. If an observer were to theorize on how a racehorse functions based solely upon that picture, it could be stated that horses fly.

This is what organizations do daily when they restrict a person's duties to what may have applied to the picture that was taken yesterday, but would be different today and will be even more different tomorrow.

**Growth is a normal process and should be welcomed. It
brings new ideas and fresh perspectives to the
organization, and enables improvement through the
infusion of needed "new blood."**

The alternative to the individual job description is
something that could be construed as a corporate or team
job description.

In essence, my department staff had developed that
description ourselves because we had a *mission. That*
mission answered the question "Why are we here?" We
were held accountable for the training, communications,
and project management functions of the corporation.

When a specific project required extra time or effort,
all of us redirected our efforts to assume responsibilities
that were not part of our formal individual job
descriptions, but which were required due to changes in
the company's operations.

This type of flexibility enabled us to feel a sense of
teamwork and camaraderie that would have been limited
had we done only what the job descriptions said we
should do. And, each new project required a new set of
responsibilities, so we were constantly tweaking the dials
to maximize our results.

**The strengths of all individuals, not job descriptions,
should determine how work is distributed.**

When you think about it, you probably do this already, violating the policies that were set up to codify what people do. The simple fact is that individuals cannot and should not be placed into boxes that were designed for someone else. To do so is to plant a time bomb that will eventually explode.

Today, management has a unique challenge that dramatically influences employee interactions. The COVID pandemic demanded that organizations reevaluate their workforces, and many individuals were asked to work from home. While at first this was viewed to be a temporary arrangement, organizations discovered operating efficiencies that had positive impacts on their bottom lines.

As a result, many people now permanently work remotely and are not required to travel to an office location. Job descriptions are either being revised or created to accommodate this restructuring. And, a significant number of permanent full-time employees are being replaced with online sub-contractors. Frequently, management is finding this to be a more flexible, cost effective way to operate.

It's difficult to build a team that is geographically dispersed, and to include non-employees in a functioning work family. Meetings via the internet cannot substitute for face-to-face contact. The concept of teamwork has taken on a new meaning.

More and more companies are scheduling periodic onsite staff meetings in attempts to bring their employees together to make personal contact that translates into meaningful work relationships. The search is still out for the silver bullet that fully solves this problem. The reality, though, is that many of these changes are now the way that business is conducted worldwide. The genie is out of the bottle and can't be put back in.

So, these are *The Basics*. The remainder of this book builds a case for creating a vibrant culture based upon them.

Chapter 5
The Staff Perspective
When is a mission not a mission?

You already know about *mission* and *vision*, so why should I waste a chapter on it? You know that every successful organization has both of these statements to guide its actions. Enough said, right? If only it was that simple. I've worn out many soapboxes on this topic and I'm not done yet. Most organizations that claim to have implemented both don't really understand what they are.

In the 1980s and 1990s, the words "mission" and "vision" became buzzwords within organizations. Companies and associations rushed to establish both so that their staffs would better understand their roles in the marketplace.

Over the next three decades, they have stuck around and are occasionally revisited, but rarely totally revised. A few words or phrases might be updated in response to new technological trends or to the increasingly large portion of the workforce working at home, yet few organizations have taken the step of starting to examine their missions from scratch.

While the initial commitment was well intentioned, it proved, in most cases, to be ineffective. The biggest reason for this was a misunderstanding of the true nature of a mission and a vision. Now that new societal and market changes have emerged, companies who have institutionalized both and need to revisit them.

A mission statement answers the question, "Why are we here?" and identifies the organization to all who look at it. A vision statement answers the question, "Where are we going?" The two together position the organization in the marketplace.

Many organizations spend an inordinate amount of time massaging the words that comprise both statements, only to arrive at "vanilla" results that can describe any number of organizations in a variety of markets. It's not the words that determine the impact.

Show Me the Mission

One of my clients, an international manufacturer of industrial products, took great pride (and spent a lot of money) formulating mission and vision statements. A large banner at the front entrance of its headquarters proclaimed the mission to the world. A tour of the inside of the building reinforced what had been done.

Prominently displayed were framed copies of the mission and vision, alongside the beliefs and values of the company. It was an unmistakable statement that this company was on the cutting edge of organizational culture. Sounds good, doesn't it?

Later, while working with the staff, I asked one of the employees about the mission. I was referred to the framed copy on the wall. "No," I said, "I'd like to ask you about the mission and how it pertains to what you do." The employee reached for his wallet and pulled out a small laminated card on which were printed the mission and vision statements. He acted as if I'd asked him a trick question. Reading it over quickly, he said, "Let's see, how *does* this apply to me?"

To him, and to undoubtedly many other employees, the formalized mission and vision were simply words that had been written down and distributed. He had neither a personal buy-in nor an understanding of what they meant. Therefore, he did not know how he contributed to what the company did for a living.

Mission and vision reflect what must be in the hearts and minds of staff members, not what's printed on a page or written on a wall.

A constant frustration to me when working to formulate effective mission statements was the attitude of many senior executives who adamantly proclaimed that their company's mission was "to make money." While shareholders would welcome this mindset, it totally negates the true function of a mission.

This focus confuses "cause" with "effect." An organization is successful and "makes money" by being good at what it does and living up to its true mission. Otherwise, why not simply find the investment that returns the greatest profit and put all of the company's capital into it? As ludicrous as this seems, it's what that statement implies.

True missions and visions are critical to success. Their impact doesn't stop once the words have been written. In fact, many successful companies have no formal written statements because both are fully understood and "lived" by the staff. They live it, so they don't have to write it down.

We Are What We Buy

Well-conceived missions, though, can really send a message to the staff about how they should perform as representatives of the company.

A national retailer once hired me to work with its staff of roughly 200 buyers whose job was to identify and purchase the stock that lined the shelves of its stores. The buyers had personal responsibility for a specific type of merchandise that complemented the retailer's image in the marketplace.

As I frequently do, I came to the session armed with a copy of the company's mission. In this case, it was a full page in length, a much longer mission than I find in most companies. It detailed the markets served by the stores, the types of consumers the stores attempted to attract, and the quality of merchandise that the stores offered. It was one of the longest mission statements I had ever come across.

At the start of session, I asked, "What is your mission?" Thinking that I would stump them, I was surprised to hear the entire group in unison recite the words of the mission that guided their actions. The buyers knew exactly who they were and what they had to do. I was impressed.

The Long and Short of It

For many years, I've served on the adjunct and professional faculties at local institutions of higher learning. In the sales and marketing courses that I teach, I stress the importance of understanding the mission and having a vision.

I've been told repeatedly by my students that mission statements must be no longer than one (or maybe two) sentences. They knew this because other consultants who'd worked with their companies told them that only short missions are memorable.

The best type of learning is personal discovery, so I regularly ask my students to bring to class the mission statements of their organizations. When they read them aloud in class, it becomes very clear that most mission statements sound alike. Only a few are distinctive enough to truly position a company as being different from its competitors.

It's not the length of the mission statement, but the impact it has on the staff, customers, and the marketplace that determines its effectiveness.

When I was retained by a large statewide association to help its board of directors restructure and upgrade the association's effectiveness, I was faced with these preconceptions about the mission statement.

The board members just stared at me when I used the existing mission as a starting point for organizational improvement. "We don't have to go over this again, do we?" I was asked.

Rather than rehash it, I led them through a total revision of the mission. The update was many times longer than the original statement. Based upon the association's *real* mission, we were then able to restructure the board and establish priorities. The board was streamlined from 35 members to 18 members, each with specific assigned responsibilities, once the board understood who the association was and why it existed.

Words are hollow if they have no real meaning and do not truly guide organizational actions. Take for example the following statement of "values" that a large American corporation proclaimed to live by.

Values

Respect: We treat others as we would like to be treated ourselves. We do not tolerate abusive or disrespectful treatment. Ruthlessness, callousness and arrogance don't belong here.

Integrity: We work with customers and prospects openly, honestly and sincerely. When we say we will do something, we will do it; when we say we cannot or will not do something, then we won't do it.

Communication: We have an obligation to communicate. Here, we take the time to talk with one another ... and to listen. We believe that information is meant to move and that information moves people.

Excellence: We are satisfied with nothing less than the very best in everything we do. We will continue to raise the bar for everyone. The great fun here will be for all of us to discover just how good we can really be.

Wouldn't you agree that, based upon the words used and the values that the company expressed, that it would be a great place to work? Isn't it clear that you'd always get honest, forthright answers from the people within the organization?

Although I have intentionally not identified companies by name in this book, the company that put together this list of values deserves to be recognized.

This is the value statement of the now-defunct Enron Corporation Some of you will recall the company that cooked the books to show a profit until its bankruptcy in 2001. For six consecutive years, *Fortune Magazine* had named it "America's Most Innovative Company." Enron had even purchased the naming rights to the Houston Astro baseball park. Little did the magazine realize how right it was with its assessment, but not in the way that it was intended.

I'll wager a consultant made a lot of money helping the company with the value statement. I wonder if anyone believed it. It's too late to find out because you all know the rest of the story, and Enron is now just a case study rather than a company.

I wonder for whom these values were *really* written. You and I both know the answer.

Chapter 6
It's All a Big Stage
Individuals play different roles

Much as players in a theatrical performance, individuals determine how they interact within the organizational culture by exhibiting the traits inherent in one of six roles.

If you've taken any sales or customer service seminars in the past, you're probably familiar with the concept of behavioral styles or personality types. In most of these courses, all people are categorized according to behavioral quadrants based upon their traits and personal characteristics.

The organizational roles that are delineated here are different. Any of the four behavioral styles can fill any of the six roles because the roles reflect the attitudes and beliefs a person exhibits within the corporate structure.

Although the roles are defined here in strict terms, keep in mind that many people within an organization *shift among two or three roles.* However, a particular prevalent role will stand out as being the one that an individual plays most often during daily encounters.

The presence of these role players and their degree of proliferation provide insights into the inner workings of any company. By understanding these individuals, strategies can be developed to target important issues, improve communications, and make needed changes.

The brief descriptions of the role players are followed by a series of *Player Profiles* in which each one is described according to a set of similar criteria. The profiles can be used as quick references to help you determine with whom you are dealing. Here are descriptions of the role players and how they act within an organization.

Player #1: The Power Player

Power Players regard the organization as a battleground with control viewed as "winning." They see most interactions as win/lose situations and try to maximize their wins. Any compromises are made with an eye toward turning concessions into future victories.

They will regard new people and ideas as opportunities for combat. Power Players will buy into someone else's changes, but will try to claim the changes as their own innovations.

Player #2: The Gatekeeper

Gatekeepers see the organization as exchanges of information and intrigues. Those who gather and channel the most of both are in control. As with Power Players, Gatekeepers like to win, but view victories in more subtle terms.

They allow others to fight their battles by selectively releasing information to those individuals who create the outcomes the Gatekeepers desire.

Player #3: The Mentor

Mentors like to take others under their wings and share information about the organization. They are willing to teach new members how to work within the structure and to maximize results.

Mentors encourage people to return so that both sides can ask questions and share current information. Mentors play win/win and judge the culture by the harmony that is exuded by coworkers. Beware: Gatekeepers often come dressed in the garb of Mentors.

Player #4: The Peer

Peers perceive all members of an organization as being equal. From the top to the bottom of the structure, they see everyone as being in the same boat and succeeding or failing together.

As a result, Peers are free with the flow of information and make no distinctions about who should be involved in decision making. Peers firmly believe that every person should have a voice in how the organization is run.

Player #5: The Worker

Workers schedule daily output based upon the known amount of work that comes into their realms of responsibility. Their comfort is in routines that have been fully learned and within which they perform well.

Workers are content to march in the same direction with the same cadence that has proven to be successful in the past. No company has ever been hurt by a "true" Worker, yet very few Workers have ever had ideas implemented because they will take "no" for an answer.

Player #6: The Glider

Gliders do enough to get by and very little else. They consider the organization to be something that must be endured to make it through life, but don't want to rock the boat lest they be placed into positions in which more may be required.

Gliders play neither win/lose nor win/win because they simply don't want to get involved in the game. Gliders want to be left alone and don't mind being regarded as outsiders.

The profiles on the following pages describe each of the role players according to the following:

Philosophy: The inner beliefs that determine how that role player views the workplace. All actions taken within the company are based upon the role player's philosophy.

View of the Organization: Described in slightly flippant terms, what comes to mind when this role player thinks of the company.

View of Coworkers: What the role player thinks of the other people within the company.

Favorite Expression: A whimsical representation of a typical phrase that might be used by this role player.

Focus: The attitude that is foremost in this role player's mind when relating to people and events within the organization.

Personal Agenda: The personal objective that underlies everything this role player does in the workplace.

Irritation: The people who drive this role player crazy.

Relationship to the Organization: What this role player would say if someone asked him or her to give a perspective on corporate life.

Player Profile
The Power Player

Philosophy: All interpersonal relationships involve power and control. The people who have the most of both will have influence and authority.

View of the Organization: A battleground.

View of Coworkers: I'll find the people who can advance my individual status, then pick their brains to find out everything I can that will help me personally.

Favorite Expression: *"Because I said so, that's why!"*

Focus: Taking advantage of opportunities to create a personal "win."

Personal Agenda: To prove that they are always right.

Irritation: People who want to play win/win.

Relationship to the Organization: As long as the company and I are in sync, I'll do anything I can to make us both successful. If I have to step on toes or make life uncomfortable for other people, then that's the way it goes. This is not a playground. It's business.

Player Profile
The Gatekeeper

Philosophy: The most effective type of control is the subtle variety. Accumulate information and carefully control its dissemination.

View of the Organization: A web of intrigues.

View of Coworkers: They all know something that I need to know to get my way. I'll pry it out of them without letting them know what I'm doing.

Favorite Expression: *"Of course you can trust me!"*

Focus: Having more information and knowing more about what's going on than anyone else in the company.

Personal Agenda: To hold everyone in the organization captive to a personal method of getting things done.

Irritation: People who won't tell them anything.

Relationship to the Organization: Certainly I want the company to succeed, but only if I'm part of the "in" crowd. Although they might not say it, people know that they must go through me to accomplish anything.

Player Profile
The Mentor

Philosophy: When one person gets better, the entire company improves. Everyone benefits when coworkers help each other to learn new skills.

View of the Organization: An extended family.

View of Coworkers: I have something to offer them, and they have something to offer me. If we teach each other how to get better, we'll all win.

Favorite Expression: *"If you don't understand something, just ask!"*

Focus: Ensuring that everyone is as knowledgeable as possible about the company and individual responsibilities.

Personal Agenda: To create an environment in which everyone can learn from everyone else.

Irritation: People who don't listen.

Relationship to the Organization: The company can benefit from my talents and experience. It feels good to be able to pass my knowledge on to someone else.

Player Profile
The Peer

Philosophy: Everyone has different skills and abilities. By working together, they can accomplish anything.

View of the Organization: A team of equals.

View of Coworkers: Job titles and job descriptions don't mean much. When something needs to get done, we'll all figure out how to complete the job.

Favorite Expression: *"Let's all pitch in and do it!"*

Focus: Emphasizing that no one is better or worse than anyone else.

Personal Agenda: To create a harmonious workplace free from tension and pressure.

Irritation: People who always want to be in charge.

Relationship to the Organization: We're all in this together, so don't confuse the issue with too much paperwork and structure. If we stay focused on what all of us can do, we'll have a company in which we all can take a great deal of pride.

Player Profile
The Worker

Philosophy: People should simply do their jobs and not get involved in aspects of the company that don't directly concern them.

View of the Organization: A series of isolation booths.

View of Coworkers: The only thing I need from them is the input that I require for my own workload. Other than that, I wish they would leave me alone.

Favorite Expression: *"Just let me do my job!"*

Focus: Shunning involvement with anything that is not specifically job-related.

Personal Agenda: To define job functions in the narrowest possible terms.

Irritation: People who want to expand the job's potential

Relationship to the Organization: The company pays me to do my job and, as long as it gets done, I shouldn't be expected to take on extra duties. We'd be better off if everyone felt this way.

Player Profile
The Glider

Philosophy: The company is where people earn money to pay for the real pleasures in life. The workplace is something that must be endured.

View of the Organization: A time-release capsule.

View of Coworkers: I know there's a way to pawn off some of my work onto other people. I'd prefer to do it in such a way that they don't even know its happening.

Favorite Expression: *"Break time!"*

Focus: Doing the smallest amount of work possible that will enable job retention without forcing job expansion.

Personal Agenda: To shrink job requirements to a minimum while maximizing free time.

Irritation: People who are enthusiastic about their work.

Relationship to the Organization: Nothing about this company can faze me. As long as I don't do anything that can get me fired, I'll survive longer than all of these people who get excited about coming to work.

While I hesitate to make this book sound too much like an academic exercise, I have observed that these role players have predictable relationships. Picture the Power Player and the Glider at opposite ends of a straight line.

To get a better handle on what I mean, take a look at the simple diagram below.

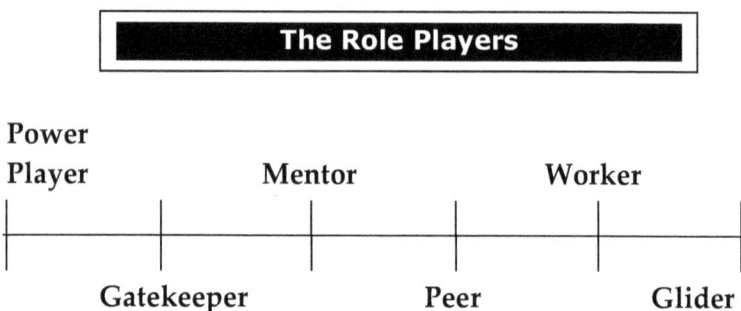

The Role Players

Power
Player   Mentor   Worker

|------+------+------+------+------+------|

      Gatekeeper   Peer   Glider

I am the first to admit that individuals bring their own values and beliefs to the table when they join a company – some of which are unalterable. Yet, I have seen too many cases in which marginal staff members have become excited about their jobs to say that people can't change.

Role Shifts

An individual can "shift" roles based upon the location of the primary role on the line. When necessary, or when changes in the organization occur, it is possible for a role player to assume the guise of either of the two closest role players to the primary role on the continuum.

For instance, a Power Player can, at times, become a Gatekeeper or a Mentor. A Mentor can play the roles of a Gatekeeper or a Peer. And a Glider, when placed in the correct situation, can become a Worker or a Peer.

You've seen this happen. When something in your organization personally affects a coworker, he or she seems to get a new lease on life and it's as if someone else showed up for work. Or if the event is perceived as negative, the coworker is more difficult to deal with.

The duration of these role shifts is based upon a variety of factors. In most cases, the shifts are short-lived and the individual reverts to the role that is most comfortable. I mentioned the word "excited." When an individual's personal hot button is pressed, he or she is more likely to continue functioning in the new role because of the personal satisfaction the new role provides.

Many studies have shown that employees choose "job satisfaction" over "monetary rewards" when rating the factors that keep them in a job. The same thing holds true when projecting how long a role shift will last.

The role shifts and reasons are, to a certain degree, predictable in the following ways.

The Power Player
To a Gatekeeper - The Power Player is relieved of some duties or reorganization takes place.

To a Mentor - The organization is functioning smoothly and the Power Player feels in control and able to share thoughts and ideas.

The Gatekeeper
To a Power Player - The Gatekeeper's usual channels of information aren't working, so he or she becomes more forceful due to frustration.

To a Mentor - The Gatekeeper is confident that he or she is "in" on everything, or the Gatekeeper fakes this role to gain more information.

The Mentor
To a Gatekeeper - Camaraderie in the workplace is threatened and the Mentor needs to find out what's happening.

To a Peer - The Mentor's instinctive helpfulness is viewed negatively by other members of the organization.

The Peer
To a Mentor - Attitudes within the organization encourage the Peer to share knowledge.

To a Worker - Coworkers rebuff the Peer's attempts at promoting harmony, or the organization frowns on the Peer's social nature.

The Worker
To a Peer - The organization "opens up" and the Worker is encouraged to utilize more skills

To a Glider - The Worker is criticized for efforts and is given no opportunity to express an opinion.

The Glider
To a Worker - The organization makes a change that personally affects the Glider in a positive way.

To a Peer - After a period of time in the role of a Worker, good things continue to happen and coworkers "pull" the Glider into a more open work environment.

The most important dynamic of these role shifts is that any player, under the right set of circumstances, can become a Mentor or a Peer.

Needless to say, these descriptions refer to observable behaviors and relationships to the organization and other employees. Online and home employees also fit into these roles, but can be more difficult to categorize.

If the remote employee's position is based solely on individual results and not on the relationship to others in the work family, management must make a decision about the value of that person in making the organization succeed.

Chapter 7
How Does Your Culture Grow?
Role players determine the culture

All organizations will have a variety of players on their staffs, but it is the authority and influence of each that become an indicator of culture. Remember: the attitudes of the people at the top of the organization will set the tone for the entire organizational structure. Their beliefs and values become predictors of the three types of corporate cultures and directly affect the role players who populate the organization.

Dominant Role Players in Top Management	Culture
Power Players *Gatekeepers*	**Control**
Mentors *Peers*	**Communications**
Workers *Gliders*	**Contentment**

The Control Culture

Power Players and Gatekeepers emphasize control. Organizations that have an abundance of these players in top positions operate in a culture that is highly competitive.

Information is guarded and kept hidden from most members because the people at the top feel as if they are the only ones who can correctly interpret what is going on. Plus, they truly believe that "ignorance is bliss" for their subordinates.

Spinning the Rumor Mill

During a project that involved implementing a major corporate change, I once encountered a Power Player corporate vice president who introduced me to his staff at a meeting for which no formal agenda had been published in advance. The vice president explained this by saying, "We didn't want to tell you what was going on because we were afraid that rumors would start."

Rumors result from little or no information being shared with all members of an organization. Especially during periods of change, people need answers.

When answers are not forthcoming, the answers are invented by staff members. The rumor mill kicks in and the reality of the change becomes distorted, invariably in a negative way.

Organizational cultures are breeding grounds for such intrigues, many stemming from the decision-maker's inability to open up and acknowledge the skills and maturity of subordinates.

The Unexpected Walk-Through

On another occasion, I was observing departmental work flow within a division of a large international corporation when the division manager approached me and told me that I must "hide" immediately. When I asked "why," he told me that the CEO's secretary had just called and the CEO was on his way over to visit the building.

Since no one had told the top executive that a consultant had been retained, I was required to stop my work until the CEO completed his walk-through. The division manager felt that my presence would be interpreted negatively. I literally hid behind a pillar until the visit was complete so as not to embarrass the manager.

Later, I found out that the panic button was traditionally pressed when senior management was present. Not only did this disrupt the work environment, but it also precluded the executive staff from realistically assessing the status of the company.

Clearing the Details

In another case, my company was contracted to write and edit the internal communications vehicle for a large service company. Suggestions for articles were provided by the client, along with the names and phone numbers of individuals who should be contacted to obtain complete information.

Invariably when my staff called to gather the details, the contacts said they needed to "clear" the conversation. Top management was consulted before these employees dared express opinions or even provide basic facts about a newsworthy company event.

Not only did the research take longer than it should have, but also the information that was shared was often sketchy and not complete enough to enable us to do a good job of writing the stories. In such cultures, information flow is jeopardized. Dominant personalities are rewarded, promoted and seen as the norm during interpersonal encounters.

Gatekeepers thrive in Control Cultures. Just as goods are bartered in a flea market, Gatekeepers barter information and knowledge.

They understand that "information is bliss" and they try to know as much as possible about everything that is happening.

Holding the Company Hostage

When working with a major national company, I encountered a Gatekeeper who held the top position in the

MIS department. He closely guarded the flow of information into his department and would only accept requests in writing after those requests had been approved by another vice president.

This procedure enabled him to control the capabilities of all facets of the company and, in effect, hold the organization hostage to his timeframes and his priorities. In addition, he knew what was happening throughout the company, because everyone utilized <u>his</u> system. In a very subtle way, the power in the company had shifted to his department because of his insistence on using a clumsy process that penalized change and innovation.

Many companies have Control Cultures that are firmly entrenched and resistant to initiatives that could make them more competitive nationally and globally. They preach the right gospel using the correct words, but their inner workings reveal that their actions contradict their words.

The Communications Culture

Mentors and Peers focus on communications. When these players permeate the management of an organization, information flows smoothly. This culture is one that fosters personal growth and readily accepts the need for change. Job titles are not as important as the people who hold those titles.

Lunch with the Boss

I was once retained for a project by a company that found a way to open communication channels. A division vice president with Power Player tendencies realized that, without meaning to do so, his natural aggressiveness caused problems when encouraging his subordinates to open up and share information. He wanted to find a way to change the culture from one which employees perceived as control to one that encouraged communications.

It became apparent that he was at his best when he didn't prepare for a presentation, but rather answered questions off the cuff in an honest, forthright manner. This informality meant that his strong behavioral traits were tempered by the excitement and enthusiasm that he expressed about the future.

The plan, then, was to put him into his comfort zone. On a weekly basis, he began sponsoring an informal "lunch with the boss." Here's how it worked.

On Monday, a sign-up sheet was placed on the company bulletin boards. Anyone who wanted to have a free lunch with the boss placed his or her name on a list. Since the lunch was limited to 10 employees (so that each could get personal attention), attendees were selectively picked from those who signed up to provide a mixture of departments and job functions. Those not selected for the current week were given priority on the following list.

On Thursday, the vice president spent the lunch hour in a meeting room at the company's plant, sharing sandwiches or pizza and soft drinks with employees, and answering any questions which came up.

At first, the attendees held back, but when it became apparent that the boss was serious about becoming a better communicator, the questions began to flow. *This Power Player had successfully shifted his role to that of a Mentor*. With that new role, a Communications Culture could take root and flourish.

The vice president enjoyed the challenge of these encounters and ended up sharing a great deal of information. In return, he understood his staff better and internal communication channels improved. His image within the division was enhanced and the lunches became a form of team building.

Any manager or executive who attempts such contact without being serious about opening up to the staff, though, will find that this process will flop miserably.

A workforce can spot a half-hearted attempt at communications from a mile away.

The Answers of the Week

For example, I was present when a company decided to open communication channels by answering employee questions, submitted through the Human Resources

Department. It was determined that two or three questions per week would be answered via responses to written queries.

Both the questions and the answers were posted on all company bulletin boards. On the surface, this seemed like a good way to promote communications. However, larger issues began to appear.

First, not all questions submitted by employees were answered. The Human Resources Department determined which items deserved a response. The issues that seemed most important to the employees were not always the ones selected by the department.

Second, the written responses that were posted were reviewed and edited by top management, often creating the impression that the answers were merely a restatement of the company line. Employees were given the same responses they had always received, the only difference being the method of delivery.

Finally, the postings were one-way communication tools with no chance for employees to ask for and receive clarification. In some cases, when employees contacted the department to ask for additional information, they were referred back to the bulletin boards where the official answers were provided. A potentially positive experience had become a negative.

Real attempts at communications are welcomed by employees and encourage involvement and innovation. Superficial communication tools serve only to reinforce employee opinions about manipulation from senior management.

The Contentment Culture

Workers and Gliders at the management level are totally agreeable to operating in a culture of contentment. Very few new ideas are instituted within that culture. Those ideas that are implemented have been tried and perfected by other organizations first, ensuring that they are safe and will not jeopardize the status quo. An example of how the Contentment Culture manifests itself can be seen in the case of a company that retained one of my associates.

The Responses Might Surprise You

The owners of the company felt that they must keep up with current management trends by hiring an outside firm to complete an internal analysis of attitudes and operations. They were confident that, even if the consultants might find a few problems, overall the owners would receive a pat on the back for the way that the business was being run. Even during a period of economic uncertainty, the company was doing moderately well.

Instead, the analysis indicated a great deal of unrest among the employees. The owners were viewed as being out of touch with day-to-day operations and refusing to share goals and projections with subordinates. Certainly the company was doing okay, said employees, but they could do a lot better if only top management would become better listeners.

The owners were presented with these results in the form of a written report delivered in person by my associate. Employee feedback was reviewed and recommendations were made. Surprised by what was found, the owners questioned the methodology and the reliability of the data.

They found reasons to explain why the results could not possibly be valid. The report was placed on the back burner and no actions were taken. They'd "always done it that way" and planned on continuing to do it that way for the foreseeable future. The Contentment Culture was firmly entrenched in the company and nothing could be done to make the owners deviate from the path they were traveling.

When a Contentment Culture permeates an organization, management finds many reasons to "not do it" and few reasons to try something new.

We Don't Need To

Another example is of a large company that jumped on the "quality bandwagon" when it was at the zenith of its cutting-edge position. The CEO proclaimed in the company's annual report that the program was being implemented. However, the vice president who was placed in charge of it told a consultant friend of mine that

"we don't use the phrase 'paradigm shift' around here."
When asked why, she said, "It doesn't apply to us."

To that company, the word "shift," meant *change,* and the
program would only apply if the company wasn't required
to make any substantial modifications to the way in which
it operated. This, of course, precluded much of what the
quality program was all about. The company's culture was
one of Contentment with no real commitment to do
anything differently.

The impetus to implement the program was simply a
reaction to a competitive marketplace that placed a great
deal of emphasis on quality. To that company, the
vocabulary of the process was a way of showing that it
was on the cutting edge. Yet, with no real substance to
back up the words, the program was meaningless from
day one.

To emphasize how buzzwords come and go, I'll wager you
haven't seen the term "paradigm shift" in years. At its
zenith in popularity, it made a lot of consultants a lot of
money.

Does One Size Fit All?

With my admitted preference for the Communications
Culture, I must place the Control Culture in the proper
perspective. Many of my friends and clients who have
started businesses smile and tell me I sound like a
consultant when I downplay the virtues of control.

Having spent three years of my life as an officer in the United States Army Signal Corps, I understand that, in certain situations, a leader doesn't have the time to solicit everyone's input before making a decision. At times, a quick summary response is what's needed to remedy an immediate problem. Yet, communications in the form of trust is required. Here's what I mean.

The Field Training Exercise

Remembering my experience in the military (the ultimate Control Culture), I realize I learned a lot about leadership, both positive and negative, by observing my fellow officers.

Once, when I was a first lieutenant and the signal officer for a firing battery, my platoon was on a field training exercise to practice the techniques we would need were we ever to be deployed in combat. Since my platoon used some fairly sophisticated equipment, the enlisted personnel were well trained and very skilled.

My personal method of running the unit was to let them be the experts and have them tell me what they required to get the job done. The battalion signal officer, on the other hand, was a captain only a few years older than me who had a different philosophy.

He once told me that to be a good officer, he felt he had to be the "best radio operator," "the best lineman," "the best crypto specialist," and "the signal expert" for the entire unit. He would regularly tell enlisted personnel how to do their jobs better and give them advice on the equipment and on their individual performance.

On this particular exercise, we were set up in the field and I entered one of the radio vans. He was there feverishly working away while my team of four radio specialists watched. He informed me (in a rather forceful tone) that the radio was not on the air yet and my radio team required his help. The team watched in silence as he checked gauges, turned dials, and reviewed manuals in an attempt to figure out what was wrong.

After about half an hour of this, he gave up, suggested I take over, and left to do something else. When he exited the van, the team leader walked over to the radio controls, turned a few dials and checked some signal levels. In less than a minute, the radio was working perfectly. He looked at me, said, "It's fixed, Sir," and the entire team broke out laughing. The captain never "got it."

Even in a Control Culture, when decisions must be made quickly and decisively, leaders must create an environment of trust in which the ideas and skills of others are appreciated and respected.

It's only when a leader respects the abilities of others that the leader earns the right to make snap judgments that generate buy-ins from staff members.

Chapter 8
The Cultural Mix
How does your organization operate?

W**hat, then, have we learned about organizational cultures? They are different, yet remarkably the same. They are unique, and yet mirror images of what takes place in other organizations. The profiles in this chapter put a structure to these cultures.

Keep in mind that your organization's culture may be a mixture. However, one of the three profiles will be MOST like your culture. Once you've identified which it is, you have a starting point for creating a vibrant culture, even when world events indicate an uncertain future.

Cultural Profiles

The profiles identify the organizational cultures according to specific categories and operational methods. Here's what you'll find:

Philosophy: The underlying belief system upon which the operations of the company are based.

Top Management: The most prevalent role players to be found in the top management of the company.

Unstated Mission: While a company may have a published mission statement consistent with current management theory and sound practice, an unstated mission exists which takes priority during periods of uncertainty.

Decision-Making Process: How decisions are made within the organization.

Motivational Climate: How employees are motivated both overtly and in subtle ways.

Employee Rewards: The attitude toward rewards and the types of rewards used by the organization.

Reaction to Change: How top management would respond if a change was proposed.

The profiles detail "pure" examples. Many organizations in transition have not yet established a definite culture.

During periods of executive reassignments and merging cultures, the specific culture that will emerge is uncertain until all of the dust settles.

Control Culture

Philosophy: The company exists as a profitable operation that will benefit those individuals who keep their noses clean and do what top management requires.

Top Management: Power Players and Gatekeepers

Unstated Mission: To make money.

Decision-Making Process: Behind closed doors with little or no input from line personnel.

Motivational Climate: Staff members are reminded of how much the company is doing for them and how lucky they are to be working for this company.

Employee Rewards: Since all people are "money motivated," financial incentives are the basic type of reward. Few, if any, recognition programs exist.

Reaction to Change: We understand the marketplace and, of course, are willing to change. But, we must ensure that the change was initiated for the right reasons by the right people. By the way, how much will it cost?

Cultural Profile
Communications Culture

Philosophy: The company is comprised of people with different skills and abilities. These must be fully utilized to provide excellent customer service in a changing world.

Top Management: Mentors and Peers.

Unstated Mission: To avoid meaningless conflict.

Decision-Making Process: Ideas and input come from all levels of the company.

Motivational Climate: The staff is self-motivated by opportunities for innovation and a free flow of opinions.

Employee Rewards: Money is not regarded as the prime motivator. Financial incentive programs are competitive, but employees are also recognized and rewarded in a variety of non-monetary ways for contributions to the company.

Reaction to Change: By keeping up with the changes in the marketplace, we are ensuring that our company will be viable in the future. We welcome change and are concerned if we do the same thing in the same way for too long.

Cultural Profile
Contentment Culture

Philosophy: The company is just fine the way it is. While others may try something new, we prefer to continue doing the things that have been successful for us in the past.

Top Management: Workers and Gliders.

Unstated Mission: To maintain the status quo.

Decision-Making Process: Based upon written rules and procedures which have worked in the past.

Motivational Climate: Praise is given only with great reluctance and is based upon longevity rather than on performance.

Employee Rewards: Compensation is structured to provide the minimum amount of financial incentives needed to maintain a workforce. Promotions and raises are infrequent.

Reaction to Change: We don't need to change. We've been successful in the past and "if it ain't broken, don't fix it." Every time we try to change, something goes wrong.

Chapter 9
The Organizational Curve
Change is a natural process

In sociology, it's called a "growth curve." In marketing, it's called a "product life cycle." In this book, we'll call it the "organizational curve." No matter which term is used, it is a method of analyzing the stages that people and organizations progress through as they advance or decline over a period of time. Here is the concept of the organizational curve.

Phase 1: Formation

A new organization is formed and is not totally certain of what it must do to ensure that it remains alive and functioning. During this period, the entrepreneurial spirit is alive and well and innovation runs rampant.

Since historical long-term norms are non-existent, the time between idea development and project completion is short. Without formal channels of communications and authority, information flows freely among all members of the organization with everyone working together to get the job done.

This type of environment generates a great deal of camaraderie and esprit. People who join the company are looking for latitude and freedom to use their talents and creativity. An organization in the Formation Phase is proactive, taking the initiative in the marketplace and basing many of its decisions upon intuition.

The Organizational Curve

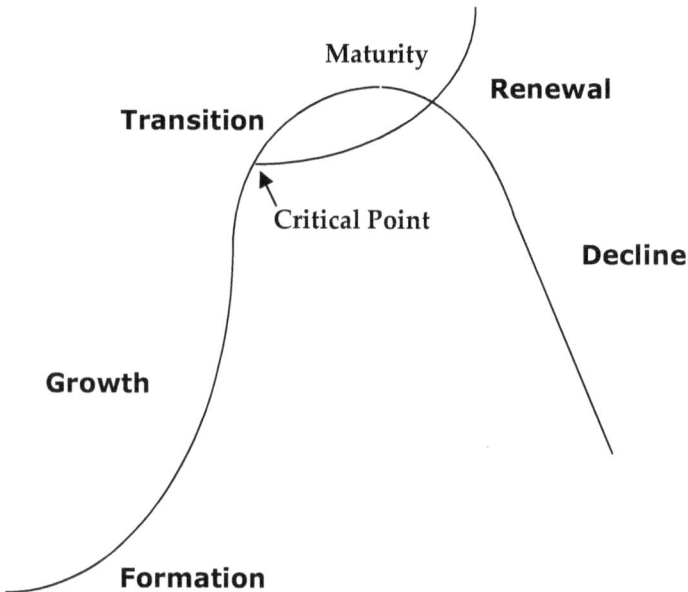

Maturity

Renewal

Transition

Critical Point

Decline

Growth

Formation

Phase 2: Growth

When an organization has established itself, an extended period of growth occurs. The organizational chart begins to develop with layers of management put in place to control specific aspects of the company.

Often, top management perceives a need for standardization, so policies and procedures are implemented that not only regulate the organization's functions, but also serve to limit responsibilities and individual initiative. Remember the section about job descriptions. It's at this point that the executive staff (or a highly paid consultant) decides that past success can only be replicated if processes and procedures are written down, formalized and published.

Because of this, the open environment of the Formation Phase can evolve into a more restrictive workplace in which more functions and duties are compartmentalized. While large organizations do require some methods for tracking and fostering continued growth, too many controls can have the opposite impact.

The company is an active player in the marketplace, but tolerates less fly-by-the-seat-of-the-pants behavior. It often establishes a system in which individuals who adopt the company line are rewarded.

Phase 3: Transition

A *critical point* signals the start of the Transition Phase. The company has been operating in a growth pattern for an extended period of time when a specific event or change in the marketplace indicates that existing operational patterns must be altered.

For instance, the product or service that the company supplies may be on the verge of becoming obsolete or internal functions may not have kept pace with the competition. Today's continuing example of this is the influence that the internet has had on global business and on personal relationships.

At that critical point, the company has a choice. It can either continue to operate in the same manner in which it has always operated, or it can make a major move to reposition itself.

The decision to change is not an easy one because the critical point occurs before the company has reached the point of *maturity* at which it will peak in profits and market share. The organization is placed in the situation of sacrificing short-term profits for long-term viability.

Not every company is prepared to make this trade-off. In fact, many companies reach the critical point and simply ignore its significance. They put Band-Aids and patches on their systems to give the appearance of change, but do not commit to meaningful, lasting organizational renewal.

Phase 4: Renewal *or* Decline

For a period of time, they will continue to be profitable and successful. However, unless they take corrective action, they will reach maturity and see a *decline* in their market share and position. Often, panic sets in and an organization takes drastic measures to return to a point at which it can a have *renewal* within the company, the same renewal that should have occurred sooner and with less reactive behavior.

When organizations are "reactive" rather than "proactive," they are more likely to implement changes that have negative rather than positive impacts.

Correlation to Culture

Specific cultures are more likely to be present during one phase of corporate growth than during another. Although the following corporate scenario is not <u>always</u> true, it is a prevalent pattern.

First, the entrepreneurial attitude of the Formation phase lends itself to the fostering of a *Communications Culture.* The free flow of ideas is essential to the new company and openness is strength in producing results and in reacting to market demands.

When the Growth Phase begins, a *Control Culture is* likely to appear. Because a company feels that it now has the proper methodology and tactics to be successful, it moves to institutionalize existing operations and to maintain internal patterns. Top management, which formerly had worked side-by-side with employees, now starts to distance itself and may throw up barriers that inhibit effective communications.

Finally, as the company moves into the Transition Phase, it can be lulled into a sense of false security and develop a *Contentment Culture.* Everything seems to function so well that no apparent need to change exists.

Unless top management steps back and reassesses the forces that currently drive the marketplace, the company can be left behind as competition stiffens with new products and services supplanting those which haven't improved.

If the organization realizes that it must react to these new demands, an interesting metamorphosis takes place. The company enters a new Phase One and undergoes a new Formation in which it must, once again, open up communication channels and rediscover the tenets that enabled it to grow and develop in the first place. This process can be observed with great regularity in today's global marketplace.

Some companies that once led their respective fields are seeing their positions decline. As a result, they are taking drastic measures to restructure and restate their missions, redefining who they are and where they want to be in the marketplace. Companies with firm grasps on the dynamics of change, understand that these measures can best be implemented if they are anticipated and planned.

That's the reason why some companies seem to be in constant states of renewal, testing products and procedures well in advance of the competition to maintain an edge in both image and sales.

Curve Compression

In the current, fast-paced global environment, timeframes are being compressed. Traditionally, the Growth Phase has lasted for a long period of time, and a critical point was not reached until the company had been in existence and operating for many years.

Today, as products and services are developed and discarded at a faster pace, the Growth Phase is shorter and shorter, and critical points occur in rapid-fire order. Projecting this operational climate into the future, it is easy to predict that soon the Growth Phase will disappear altogether with a company constantly in transition while reforming its operations to remain viable.

The only culture which can handle a constant barrage of critical points and renewals is the Communications Culture.

With the current focus on a global marketplace in uncertain times, ideas must be exchanged easily and effectively. As a product reaches the consumer, it is already obsolete and being replaced by one, two or three new generations of the same product already under development.

When ideas can flow without restrictions, and improvements can be made without negative ramifications, an organization can move from Formation to Transition to Formation smoothly.

The Communications Culture is populated by an abundance of Mentors and Peers. By their actions and their demeanors, they promote the proactive type of involvement needed to function effectively in the compressed curve. This means that successful organizations must foster the development of Mentors and Peers to ensure long-term viability.

Under the right set of circumstances, any of the role players can become either a Mentor or a Peer. The job of managers and executives, then, is to create an environment that enables these shifts to occur so that the Communications Culture becomes a natural outgrowth of the attitudes and beliefs of all members of the organization.

Chapter 10
Prescriptions
What do we do now?

If your organization is not structured to accept the requirements of the Communications Culture, strategies can be implemented which will enhance existing efforts and refocus an organization. They serve as prescriptions for symptoms that might prove to be fatal for some organizations.

Prescription #1:
Communicate with each other.

This sounds so simple, but it is surprising how many top managers and executives position themselves behind closed doors with access to them limited to a few select individuals. When this happens, the entire staff follows the example, erecting both physical and mental barriers that block effective communications, a real-life application of Basic #1.

The executives who know the most about what is happening in their companies are those who spend the time fostering ongoing creative dialogue with employees. While some regard this as a distraction, others understand that it shortens the time that must be spent in research and problem solving. The staff is a built-in R&D department whose resources can be tapped for the betterment of the entire organization.

Walking the Floor

I once worked with a top executive who ensured that
every employee was given a nameplate to be displayed in
his or her work area. In addition to enhancing the prestige
of the job, it allowed the executive to call everyone by
name.

When he visited one of his company's facilities, he
"walked the floor", greeting people personally. Because
his demeanor and manner were warm and genuine,
employees would tell him about potential problems, large
and small, which could affect the organization.

Some of these problems would never have been channeled
to him by middle managers because, to them, the problems
would have seemed insignificant.

**The executive's ability to communicate with the staff
allowed him to squelch small problems before they
became big ones.**

Contrast this to another executive whose office was located
one floor above 150 of his corporate line employees. Many
of them didn't even know what he looked like because he
conducted most of his meetings in his corner office.

When he needed to see someone, his secretary would call
and set up the appointment for him. Very rarely did he
speak to anyone below the level of middle management.
As a result, the problems that reached his desk were all big

ones, even the ones that had started off as small and quickly solvable.

I can't help but think of the CEO of BP who answered questions from American lawmakers about the massive oil spill in the Gulf of Mexico. His answers were: "I'm not a scientist," "I'm not an engineer," "I'm not a construction worker," etc., etc. This was interspersed with an abundance of "I didn't know" responses.

Although he didn't formally say what he *was*, it became apparent to all who heard him that he was out of the loop when it came to knowing what was really going on in his company. No one expected him to know everyone's job intimately, but what was rightly expected was that he knew what was going on. Perhaps if he had been more involved with *wanting* to know the real facts, the disaster could have been averted. Within a very short time, he had left the company to "pursue other interests."

To help determine if your company communicates well, informally track the time staff members spend emailing each other and writing memos versus the number of times two employees solve a problem either face to face or via the telephone.

Memos and emails are one-way communications. They do not lend themselves to reaching quick, reliable solutions to organizational problems. Although email has replaced almost all of what used to be in memos, in corporate

America memos are still written, but not always for the right reasons.

Don't Ask Questions, Just Do It

While working in the corporate world, my immediate boss was a senior vice president with no predictable office schedule. Because he always seemed to have other priorities, meaningful dialogue with his direct-reports was infrequent.

To compensate for this, he would write memos, many of them only two or three sentences long. Often, he would write a string of separate memos to the same person on the same day, each addressing a different topic.

Consider the amount of time spent on this effort. First, the senior VP would dictate the memos to his secretary. Then, she would word process them. He would be given copies to proofread.

His secretary would make the corrections. The final versions would be produced for signature. Then (rather than use internal company mail), the secretary would hand-deliver the memos to the addressees.

The most significant aspect of this management style, though, was the end result. By the time the memos were delivered, the senior VP had left for the day. This meant that those of us who received the memos weren't able to respond immediately. We either had to wait until he was available in his office, or respond with memos of our own.

And memos breed faster than rabbits. One memo
produces two, which produces three, ad infinitum
If the boss had simply picked up the phone and carried on
a real dialogue for ten minutes with each of his
subordinates, the lengthy paper trails would have been
avoided.

Even with email, memos are still ingrained in some
organizations. Memos serve larger (and often more
nefarious) functions than simply to inform. First, they
enable management to issue directives without having to
listen to feedback about the effects of the policies. Second,
copies are often sent to a string of other individuals who
are made aware of the content of the memos.

While this may help disseminate information to other staff
members, it can also serve as a "warning" to the memo
recipients that others in the organization are also aware of
the contents. The same warning applies to emails that are
printed out and kept in files.

Finally, memos are used as historical records that can be
dragged out at a later date to prove that a person really did
say what he or she purports to have said. (The initials CYA
come to mind. Ask around - you'll find someone who
knows what they mean.) Sound communications with
effective feedback is supplanted by a system that promotes
intrigue and limits input.

While some would argue that time limitations preclude
one-on-one conversations or small group meetings, my

experience is that companies that communicate in person actually save time because problems are solved quickly and "office cliques" are less likely to develop.

A feeling of unity is promoted and fewer roadblocks are erected against new ideas when they have been talked out in advance.

Prescription #2:
Establish a meaningful mission.

While mission and vision were discussed previously, they deserve to be revisited. The pivotal word in this prescription is "meaningful." Many companies have mission statements that are posted on walls and discussed in employee handbooks, but the missions are not living, breathing parts of the organizational culture.

A real mission is developed with staff members from all levels who understand what is happening within the organization. As mentioned before, it answers the question, "Why are we here?"

What was stated earlier deserves emphasis. Don't make the error of answering this question with "to make a profit." If the stated mission is "profit," then employees simply perform the activities that will produce an immediate monetary benefit to the company without regard for the long-term effect of what they are doing.

Many customer service functions and public relations programs would be excluded because, by buying into this so-called mission, the staff takes the most expeditious path toward generating revenue.

While understanding that companies will cease to exist if they do not make money, profitability is not the essential reason for existence. A mission is so much more than the bottom line on a balance sheet. It provides the standards by which the company does business and gives direction and purpose to the entire organization.

It is surprising how many companies have a formal system of job descriptions, but have never implemented a meaningful mission. I refer to this as the "Roman galley" method of operation. Think about the analogy.

Roman Galley Management

The galleys roamed the Mediterranean Sea, both for commerce and for conquest. Those unlucky enough to be kidnapped by the Romans became slaves whose sole jobs were to pull oars when a drum was sounded. The cadence of the drum determined the speed of the galley.

To those in command, the only information the slaves required was how fast to row at a particular moment. The galley slaves didn't need to know why the speed was required or where the ship was traveling. The Romans who were in charge knew. That was good enough.

Unfortunately, some executives and managers still operate this way. They say, "I know what the mission is and that's good enough. You just do your job as it's described and everything will be fine." When it's not fine, employees are blamed for lack of initiative and failure to follow orders.

A true mission is a reflection of who the company is in the marketplace and the standards by which it conducts business. It leads to the vision that the company has for the future. It provides the hook on which employees can hang their hats and feel pride in their work efforts.

Although I question certain aspects of the functionality of job descriptions, the thought process of top management is called into focus here. To institute job descriptions without having a mission is like training a crew to sail a boat, but not telling them where they are going.

They may be good at the skills of their individual jobs, but without a destination, they could end up in any port – and feel as if they did their jobs the way they were trained to do them. As the saying goes, "If you don't know where you're going, any road will get you there." And, any road you take will, by extension, be the right road.

A meaningful mission creates the buy-in that is required for the entire organization to set the company's course together. Then, each person's efforts assume a new worth and dignity as, quite literally, everyone is in the same boat. 85

Prescription 3:
Resolve problems immediately.

Once an effective system of communications has been implemented within the company, potential problems will come to the forefront quickly. This should not be regarded as a negative for the company. On the contrary, it is a huge positive.

Perceived problems will always be present within organizations, whether or not employees feel that they are able to open up to management to discuss the problems.

By getting them out in the open and placing them on the table, they can be addressed and circumvented before small problems become big ones. Think of the benefits. Sparks can be stamped out before they become raging forest fires. In addition, the workforce feels attached to the executive staff because its opinions are actively solicited.

HOWEVER - and this is a monumental "however" - any problems which are identified must be acted upon immediately. The surest way to slam a door that is slowly being opened is to ignore what is on the other side of the door.

Employee concerns, even those which may seem small in the overall context of the company, must result in some sort of action that can help solve the problem.

This doesn't mean that the problem will be immediately solved. It means that the individuals who perceived that the problem existed must see movement and a truthful attempt to address the situation.

If that occurs, a snowball effect begins to take place. Employees see that management is serious about open communications, so more and more potential problems are revealed, leading to increased dialogue and problem resolution at an earlier point.

What do you <u>really</u> want to know?

A large company with which I once worked decided that it wanted to tap the opinions of its people via small group meetings. A system was developed which enabled employees to meet on a regular basis with a format for identifying operational concerns and requirements for improvement. (Remember "quality circles"? Another revolutionary concept that we no longer hear about.)

Since the company had never done something like this before, employees were uncertain about the process and looked for a hidden agenda. After a few meetings, though, they began to get excited because, for the first time, their opinions were being actively sought with the promise of action.

They met their responsibilities and gave management a list of suggestions that they felt could make the company operate more smoothly. The excitement that was generated could have renewed the company with an invigorated workforce, were it not for management's reaction to the suggestions.

The list was reviewed and, behind closed doors, the executive staff determined that the employee input was "not what we were looking for." Word was sent back to the groups to "try again." and come up with something that management could buy into.

The reaction was predictable. Employees felt as if they had been duped. They had done their parts and lived up to their obligations, but management had ignored their efforts. And, employees asked, what was management looking for?

Did it want real input or a rubber stamp of its own policies? Needless to say, the effort died a quick death when employees saw neither rewards nor resolution for problems as a result of their efforts.

Yet, the potential was there for the employees to have made a positive impact on the company for the long-term if only top management would have realized that <u>all</u> problems or suggestions for improvement are significant and deserve immediate attention and action.

When people are treated as valued and knowledgeable members of the company, they continue to provide input and information that can be used to benefit the entire organization.

When their problems are ignored and they see no respect or regard for their thoughts, they become adversaries and the company cannot reach its full potential.

Prescription #4:
Write down the unwritten rules.

Every organization has these unwritten rules, but it is their nature and prevalence that determine their impact. What do I mean by "unwritten?" Many procedures and relationships in a company exist by innuendo and inference, not by edict.

I Have the Marker

For example, a senior manager I once worked with was known as an individual who always wanted to have "the marker in his court." If another person did a favor for him, it would be repaid immediately. In that way, he could quickly call in his markers to get around the formal company channels.

Everyone knew that he functioned in this way, yet the unwritten rule was that you stayed in his good graces because of his power within the company. All the while, you realized that you would be expected to respond speedily to his requests.

Was this a written rule? Of course not! Was it a rule? Without a doubt! Did it have an impact on the functioning of the organization? You'd better believe it did!

These unwritten rules often take precedence over the written rules. They are based upon interpersonal relationships that underlie much of what occurs within the company.

Use *My* Purchase Order

Another example of an unwritten rule would be the case, mentioned briefly in the section about the Control Culture, of the MIS executive who superseded the purchase order system of the company. If you recall, when a department wanted to buy a new piece of computer equipment or application software, a request was submitted and cycled through the company to obtain the correct sign-offs.

Eventually, the request ended up on his desk. He was expected to coordinate the purchase at the best possible price and deliver it to the requesting department.

However, the unwritten procedure was different. If the executive wasn't consulted in advance of the request, the purchase would not be made. Even if the CEO signed the purchase order, he would find a reason for delaying delivery.

The roadblock was erected to send a signal to everyone in the company that he had the power to help or hurt anyone unless his individual rules were adhered to.

When these "rules" are written down, they become less nebulous and more concrete. When pulled into the cool

light of day by the reality of the written word, they take on
a different appearance. Until they are acknowledged, they
will not be changed because no one will admit that they
even exist.

Once they are down on paper, it is up to the organization
to conduct its own problem-solving sessions, examining
what's happening and taking actions that are designed to
smooth the way for operational reform. Honesty is a
prerequisite for this process.

**Unless the unwritten rules are stated, their existence is
denied. The fear of offending powerful people or of
jeopardizing the status quo will make some companies
veer off-course and give only lip service to this
prescription.**

Those who do formalize the informal will find new
insights to the inner workings of their companies and to
the people who must live with their impacts.

Prescription #5:
Corral the "sacred cows".

Belief systems that have hung around for years are the
"sacred cows" of any organization. Many times, they exist
solely because they have always been there. Belief systems
aren't necessarily bad – nor are they necessarily good.
That's why they must be corralled and brought into an
"enclosed area" where they can be looked at closely to
determine what significance they have in today's
marketplace.

When you do this, expect predictable reactions from certain members of your staff. Those who have operated for years according to the wanderings of these sacred cows will defend them to the hilt.

Take a Ride on the Railroad

A good example is the sacred cow that hung around the railroad industry from the 1800s until relatively recently. The industry believed it was only a "railroad" and that customers who used its services were purchasing "rail services." As the lead person in a consulting project with a major railroad, it was imperative that that mindset change for the organization to be renewed.

On the Organizational Curve, you'll recall that, when the critical point is reached, an organization's actions determine renewal or decline. If the decision to change is postponed, whatever is done becomes "reactive" rather than "proactive" and extremely painful.

Sadly to say, many of America's railroads didn't realize that they had become "transportation companies" to the marketplace. While, in the past, they had only been concerned about competing with other railroads, they were now going up against air freight and over-the-road delivery companies who could, in many cases, do the job better and more cost effectively than the railroads.

Added to this were the organizational structures of the railroads themselves. Job titles and (gulp!) job descriptions still reflected the traditional way of operating. And, many older employees who'd grown up with that sacred cow were resistant to altering the ways in which they'd always done business.

Fortunately, I was working with an executive staff that realized something had to be done quickly or the company would have serious problems. The real challenge was getting that message to the staff. It took hard work and perseverance to get everyone to buy in to what the railroad had become.

In reality, some of the staff members never did buy in. A significant number of the long-term employees decided to retire rather than to leave their comfortable sacred cow behind. Some people were so set in their habits and job functions that, for their own reasons, they refused to adapt. A parting of the ways then became the most desirable result for everyone.

The manner in which these individuals are treated as they exit the organization will affect the company's image in the marketplace. They should be thanked for their past contributions and supported in their decisions about the future. If they leave with sour tastes in their mouths, they will spread the word that they were treated unfairly and that the organization doesn't take care of its staff.

When sacred cows are corralled and discarded, attrition will occur. Expect it and use it as a catalyst to infuse new ideas into the organization.

When the new blood has no attachment to the old, accepted ways of doing business, it can be the change agents for the required renewal.

Prescription #6:
Compress the organizational chart.

This isn't a euphemism for "downsizing," or (a term that is now in vogue) "rightsizing." It is, instead, a legitimate strategy to position the top levels and line employees of a company closer together.

All of us have gone through an exercise in which information is given to someone in a group. That person whispers the information to someone else who, in turn, relays it to another person.

After several more people are added to the loop, the last person to receive the information is asked to tell the entire group what was said. Invariably, the details have changed. Often, the alterations make the information useless or even contradictory to what was said in the first place.

This is what happens when employee thoughts and ideas are filtered through multiple levels of management. The original messages may have had been pertinent to the company, but they are modified, adjusted, and seemingly made more palatable as they progress through the organizational chart. The end result becomes a diluted substitute for the real content.

Multi-Level Management

Levels of management are especially abundant in Control Cultures. In particular, Power Players who are top executives like to limit the number of people who can regularly access them.

In many respects, the bestowal of the right to enter the executive's office is an unwritten reward that is given only to a few individuals. It is one of the trappings of prestige that is intrinsic within the Control environment.

What this does, of course, is take the decision-makers farther and farther away from the people who have the most knowledge of day-to-day corporate operations. The sanitized versions of company happenings misrepresent potential problems and produce misdirected solutions.

An active Communications Culture management style demands that top management get closer to the line workers in the organization. This is inherently a more trusting relationship and one that requires fewer levels of review in order for an idea to be implemented.

Reaching the point at which the organizational chart is compressed will not be easy. In many companies, the existing organization is the result of fiefdoms that formed as the company advanced through a Growth Phase.

The most desirable culture for today's time of uncertainty is one that establishes and promotes Mentors and Peers.

This means compression must take place to put the entire organization on the same path with the same goals and understanding of what is needed to be successful.

Prescription #7:
Use, but don't overuse, technology.

Email and texting have revolutionized the way managers and executives run their departments and companies. All of us are able to be in constant contact with people around the world and decisions are made at lightning speed – often to the detriment of the decision-maker.

By all means, use technology or you'll be left behind. Yet, as the old adage professes, "It's people who get things done." The overuse of technology dehumanizes the organizational environment and can mask important behind-the-scenes facts from those who must make decisions.

When employees feel as if they are faceless numbers or replaceable parts, they are divorced from the organization and feel no obligation to live by the "rules" or to make suggestions for improvement.

This is when a sinister form of protest rears its head. Employees with no commitment or allegiance to the company can "sabotage" its operations. This frequently happens when older employees feel as if they are being forced out. Sometimes the origins of words tell more about their meanings than the current usage.

Grinding to a Halt

The word *sabotage* came into existence during the Industrial Revolution in France. People who were used to working in the fields flooded the cities to find jobs in the factories and earn more money than they could by farming the land.

Most of the rural workers couldn't afford leather shoes, so they wore wooden shoes, which also made it easier to move about in the farm fields. The factories of that era had large gearing to put everything in motion. So, when the workers wanted to punish management and shut down the factory, they would simply throw their wooden shoes, called "sabot," into the gears.

When the gears ground to a halt, the factory could no longer operate and the workers got their revenge on management by "sabotaging" the entire operation. Because of the digital world in which we now live, sabotage can be both subtle and pervasive.

When the workplace becomes impersonal and detached from the individual, he or she feels less remorse in not fully buying into what the company is selling, and sees no problem in wasting time or not living up to expectations.

Just Think About It

Texting has become a prevalent means of communication both in our personal and in our business lives. It is convenient and easy to use, yet its most-attractive attribute, speed, also presents its greatest problem. Yes, it's true - some messages require a response either of only a few words, or of an ever-present emoji.

How often, though, have you transmitted your reply before thoroughly thinking it through and, after only a few seconds, wish you would have written something different or could take it back?

Response without analysis can cause misinterpretations and misunderstandings leading to hard feelings and multiple follow-up messages. Texts, as with emails, have no emotion, inflection, or clarification. Put yourself on the receiving end of your texts and determine if they really say what you want them to convey.

Nothing takes the place of one-on-one dialogue with employees. They truly determine the viability of the company.

Technology is a tool, not a substitute for understanding the workforce and creating buy-ins to a meaningful mission and vision. A warning! During uncertain, turbulent times, it is not unusual for management to fall back into patterns that have been practices in the past. Often, a Control

Culture is re-instituted in an organization until the "crisis" is over.

As a former Army officer, I can understand and appreciate the need for a Control Culture in certain situations. In a battle zone, little time exists to discuss critical decisions. When belt-tightening occurs, many organizations treat their markets as battle zones and their staff members as soldiers who should simply obey orders.

While this may work in a war, it has a different type of impact in an organization. It may be viewed as a necessary measure to ensure viability, but it will not serve the long-term needs of the organization. When the staff members have a chance to leave, they will go where they have a say and an internal commitment to what is going on.

A Communications Culture, then, is even more vital today than it has been in the past if an organization is to navigate through a dynamic global marketplace.

Summary
What all of this really means

In the final analysis, no book or consultant can make a lasting difference in any organization unless people in that organization feel involved in its daily operations.

The biggest roadblock to this happening is the failure of executives and senior managers to look in the mirror and to honestly assess their personal impact upon what is going wrong. It is common for the people in those positions to reinforce each other's actions and to shift responsibility for failures to other staff members or outside events over which they have no control.

If Only Everyone Was Like Me

A big reason why this occurs is that managers tend to hire people who are similar in outlook to themselves. Think about the way in which you hire or the way in which your company pinpoints new employees.

Rather than find out what is needed, is the focus on finding someone who is "just like us"? If so, needed talents and viewpoints might be getting locked out of ever reinvigorating your organization.

The perspective given here is meant to stimulate thoughts that can create strategies for improvement by providing a framework on which to hang the feelings and observations that are rampant within all organizations.

It is the personal commitment and desire for improvement, coupled with excitement for the future that determines the ultimate survival of any organization.

A new global marketplace of interdependence is upon us. Organizations that look at themselves, understand their cultures, and "tweak the dials" to improve performance will assume the leadership positions in a fast-paced worldwide economy, even in uncertain times.

Analyze Your Culture

To help my clients categorize their organizational cultures, I've developed *The Cultural Analysis*, a tool for taking the first step in understanding what is happening.

It's not magic! It's simply a method of recording what you come in contact with in the workplace daily. Here's how I came up with the design.

As an individual who has worked in and around organizational structure for over 30 years, I have been an observer of the ways in which people act and interact in organizations. After being inside my clients' doors for a relatively short period of time, I began to mentally categorize the culture of each organization based upon the subtle cues which are given by staff members.

When other people asked me how I could make this categorization so quickly (and fairly accurately), I realized that the most basic clues were the words which people in the organization used when describing how they do business.

The 19 Organizational Belief Statements

To formalize this process, I listed all of the statements which gave me information about the culture. My list numbered about 60 such statements. My goal was to create an instrument that could provide a practical, simple look at culture. So, I pared the list down to 19 statements that, if heard, give an immediate perspective on how that organization's culture functions.

The statements are all reflections of what I refer to as "organizational beliefs" which start with top management, filter through the organization, and create an operational environment. The 19 items on the instrument are scored in relation to the *Control, Communication* and *Contentment Cultures*.

If you want it today, it can be purchased and downloaded at: www.cultural-analysis.com.

A hard-copy version, *The Cultural Analysis Kit for Trainers and Facilitators*, is available at most e-stores, including Amazon.

Feel free to can contact me at:

Management Strategies, Inc.
PO Box 191
Cedarburg, WI 53012
(262)377-7230

jack@pachuta.com

Seminars and Workshops
From Jack Pachuta

How to Create a
VIBRANT CULTURE
in Uncertain Times

Based on concepts in this book, the program focuses on the organizational structures which are key to the implementation of a vibrant organization, promoting buy-ins to far-reaching initiatives.

Organizational Players
Much as the players in a theatrical performance, people determine how they will cope within the structure by exhibiting the traits inherent in one of six roles. Learn how to categorize these players and determine how their attitudes affect the organization.

How Companies Evolve
Over time, all organizations change. By tracking a company's past, predictions can be made about its future. Learn how to understand the trends that exist within organizations, determining how they affect current operations, then making logical plans for growth and new opportunities.

Organizational Structures
Structures develop based upon the attitudes and beliefs of the people who hold power within organizations. Learn to recognize the clues providing insights to internal functioning.

Organizational Cultures
The culture of an organization can be categorized in one of three ways, each culture having its own philosophy and operational methods. Learn to understand corporate culture and its impact on the organization.

Mission and Vision
Without a realistic, goal-driven mission, a company cannot have a vision. Without the correct vision, the organization will not be successful. Learn what they are and why both are necessary.

Motivational Climates
Within the organization, a climate exists which determines how individuals are treated and attitudes formed. Learn how culture affects motivation.

Effective Organizational Concepts
To instill a common mission and vision throughout the organization, certain essential concepts must be grasped and viewed as the norm. Learn what the "gurus" say about successful programs and find out how their ideas can become part of daily operations.

Prescriptions for Improvement
Once a commitment for improvement is made, enabling the culture to be more receptive to new ideas, an organization must develop a cohesive plan. Learn to follow a list of prescriptions that improves the environment in which change is implemented.

Personal Action Plan
Any program is only as good as the results it produces. Learn to develop personal action plans which will be used to chart individual actions and results.

How to Manage Change
While Building an Effective Team

In a fast-paced, changing global marketplace, people must expand beyond traditional methods. This program stresses new concepts for goal-setting and leadership. Topics include:

The Nature of Change

Change is a natural process that can prompt revitalization in individuals and systems. Maturity and full potential can only be realized through a process of development, growth, adjustment, and renewal. Learn to better understand the role of change in everyday life and to find opportunities for making change a positive experience.

The Effects of Change

Differences among people and organizations mean that change can have both beneficial and destructive results. While frequently frustrating, change can ensure long-term viability. Learn how to identify and react to the emotional and physical effects of change.

How People React to Change

During a period of fast-paced change, people can be categorized according to their willingness to try something new. Learn to identify personal feelings about the changes, and to develop strategies for working with all affected individuals.

Coping with Resistance

Resistance is an expected part of the change process. When it is anticipated, it can be managed and its effects minimized. Learn the causes of resistance and how to analyze its unique impact upon each individual.

The "Self-Talk" of Change

A person's internal perception of what is happening determines whether or not planned changes will be accepted or rejected. Learn how altering the "self-talk" can alter the outcome, and learn to master techniques which predict internal motivation based upon external cues.

Change Facilitators

Specific actions and attitudes on the part of management will change perceptions and speed the staff's acceptance of change. Learn what an organization's decision-makers can do to ease tensions in a changing work environment.

Implementation Strategies

A realistic appraisal of change is the first step toward developing a comprehensive implementation plan which must include communications, opportunities for feedback, and a method for modification. Learn how to ensure that everyone fully understands and "buys in" to proposed changes.

Action Plan

Any program is only as good as the results it produces. Learn to develop personal action plans which will be used to chart individual actions and results.

How to Negotiate as if
Your Success Depends on It

Providing valuable insights and hands-on practice for
win/win negotiations, this program emphasizes the skills
required to work with others to achieve excellent results.
Topics include:

Key Negotiation Concepts
Any action taken during negotiations must be based upon
three fundamental concepts that form a foundation for the
entire process. Learn to approach a negotiations
opportunity with the proper mindset.

Power Factors
Before beginning negotiations, seven factors determine
who has intrinsic power. Learn how to predict each side's
power base and use them in a win/win environment.

Strategies and Tactics
To maximize results, negotiators must understand and
utilize the right combination of planned actions. Learn 17
specific strategies and tactics along with their purposes
and counters.

Guidelines for Concessions
Often negotiators must concede certain points in order to
benefit their positions in other areas. Learn the psychology
of concessions along with seven guidelines.

Questioning
Gathering the correct information is at the core of good negotiations. Learn when to ask questions, the types of questions to ask, and how to handle difficult questions directed at you.

Listening Skills
Information is gathered and interpreted most effectively when good listening skills are practiced. Learn to identify and control communications by becoming an active listener.

Players in the Negotiations Game
The behavior styles of individuals have a marked impact on the overall negotiations plan. Learn how to categorize the personality styles of the negotiators into four quadrants.

Relationship Strategies
Each personality style must be handled differently to facilitate agreement. Learn how to best address the unique characteristics of the negotiators.

Alternatives at an Impasse
When agreement cannot be reached, well-defined actions can get the negotiations back on track. Learn 11 creative alternatives that can be used when an impasse occurs.

Negotiating on the Telephone
Contact via telephone presents its own challenges to a negotiator. Learn what makes telephone contact unique, as

well as seven techniques for maximizing telephone negotiations.

Body Language
Non-verbal communications can reveal a great deal about another person. Learn the meaning of certain gestures and actions.

Team Negotiations
A team of negotiators must be prepared to mesh their activities into a cohesive position. Learn how to select a negotiating team and utilize tactics that have an impact on the outcome.

Positioning and Room Arrangement
Certain physical items can help determine success. Learn how to arrange the conference room and position your team at the negotiations table.

Handling Difficult Negotiators
On occasion, personalities can get in the way of agreement. Learn how to handle hostile remarks and ultimatums while avoiding defensiveness.

Negotiating from a Weak Position
When a particular position requires more strength, negotiators must be able to modify their actions. Learn to understand the "big picture" while keeping a positive mental attitude.

Common Negotiating Errors

Negotiators must avoid certain errors to remain on track. Learn the nine most common negotiating errors while applying the "slight-edge" principle.

About the Author

For over four decades, **Jack Pachuta** has been a consultant, trainer, and speaker, working with organizations on three continents.

As the field director of the first interactive use of cable television in North America, he helped change the way mass media is perceived.

As a vice president of a corporation named one of Forbes Magazine's "200 Best Small Companies," he headed its training, communications, and project management functions.

A graduate of Kent State University, Jack is a Vietnam Era Veteran, having served as an officer in the United States Army Signal Corps. He later was a senior field tech for Northrop Corporation, compiling data about the Pershing Nuclear Missile System used by the Joint Chiefs of Staff to evaluate tactical operations in Europe.

Holding masters degrees from the University of Southern California and Michigan State University, Jack has served on the adjunct and professional faculties of many colleges and universities in the Milwaukee area.

Currently, the president and owner of Management Strategies, Inc., in Cedarburg, Wisconsin, Jack works with his clients to improve their organizational culture, communications, and negotiation skills.

His clients have included Jockey International, ShopKo Stores, Maytag, Satellite Industries, Pepsico, Kaytee Products, Thomson Audio Hong Kong, the Asia Pacific Institute for Management Development in Singapore, Multi-Finance in Athens, Greece, Connex of Romania, and many more.

Jack met his English wife, Renira, over breakfast in Portugal while they were both living in Germany. They now have two daughters, a cat, and a house next to a Christmas tree farm in southeastern Wisconsin.

Jack is a past president of the Wisconsin chapter of the National Speakers Association. He is also a mystery writer and artist, and a member of the Cedarburg Artists Guild and the League of Milwaukee Artists.